AFRICA'S SOUL HOPE

2007-8 NMI
MISSION EDUCATION RESOURCES

✳ ✳ ✳

BOOKS

AFRICA'S SOUL HOPE
The AIDS Crisis and the Church
by Ellen Decker

BABOONS ON THE RUNWAY
And Other Humorous Stories from Africa
by Richard Zanner

MEETING JESUS
by Keith Schwanz

THE NUDGE IN MY SIDE
Stories from Indonesia and the Philippines
by The Bob McCroskeys

THEY SAW ONLY FEET
More Life Lessons from Missionary Kids
by Dean Nelson

A LOVE STORY FROM TRINIDAD
by Ruth O. Saxon

✳ ✳ ✳

ADULT MISSION EDUCATION RESOURCE BOOK

RESPONDING TO MISSION CHALLENGES
Editors: Aimee Curtis and Rosanne Bolerjack

AFRICA'S SOUL HOPE

the AIDS crisis and the church

ellen decker

Nazarene Publishing House
Kansas City, Missouri

Copyright 2007
Nazarene Publishing House

ISBN-13: 978-0-8341-2289-5
ISBN-10: 0-8341-2289-8

Printed in the United States of America

Editor: Aimee Curtis
Cover Design: Darlene Filley
Interior Design: Sharon Page

10 9 8 7 6 5 4 3 2 1

DEDICATION

To Ryan, Jason, and Kevin,
sons who bring great gladness,

"The father of a righteous man has great joy;
he who has a wise son delights in him.
May your father and mother be glad;
may she who gave you birth rejoice!"
Proverbs 23:24-25

and to the people of Swaziland,
whom I also love

CONTENTS

REV. ELLEN GAILEY DECKER

is an ordained elder in the Church of the Nazarene. She has served in a variety of pastoral, missions, and writing roles at the local, district, and general church levels. An MK (missionary kid) from Swaziland, Africa, Ellen has lived on three continents and traveled to almost 30 countries, more than half of those have been in Africa.

Ellen is the author of the book, *The Power of One,* published in 2006. She has been published in *Today's Christian Woman, WORLD, Virtue, World Mission, Holiness Today,* and *Come Ye Apart/Reflecting God.* Ellen has written for various NMI publications, and edited the most recent *Faith Promise Planner.* Several of her anecdotes have been published in Liz Curtis Higgs's books. Ellen is the founding editor of *Nazarene Compassionate Ministries* magazine.

Her life-verse is from Acts 20:24, "I consider my life worth nothing to me, if only I may finish the race and complete the task the Lord Jesus has given me—the task of testifying to the gospel of God's grace."

Her favorite quote is from Mother Teresa: "We are all pencils in the hands of a writing God, who is sending a love letter to the world."

Ellen and her husband, Hank, are blessed by their children: Ryan and his wife, Kendra; Jason; Kevin; and five sponsored kids in South Africa, Zambia, Democratic Republic of Congo, and Zimbabwe.

ACKNOWLEDGMENTS

In memory of Rev. Phineas Bresee, a founding member of the Church of the Nazarene, for outlining so eloquently our purpose: "Let the Church of the Nazarene be true to its commission; not great and elegant buildings; but to feed the hungry and clothe the naked, and wipe away the tears of sorrowing, and gather jewels for His diadem."

* * *

With deep gratitude to all the people who shared their souls and whose names and stories are in these pages.

Thanks to all who sent information or photographs, prayed, encouraged, or helped with logistics for Africa trips: Chuck and Doris Gailey, Carol Holt, Sharon Lee, David Malinzi, Elizabeth Musimbi, Mary Magagula, Sharon Kessler, Célestin Chishibanji, Suzanne Wilson, David Park, Bill Dawson, Petros Pato, Karen Butt, Lynn Shaw, Joyce Cole, Irene Nangobi, Elias Muigai, Fran Gailey, Cynda Kindle, Paul Whitaker, Bob Prescott, Evie Gardner, Wellington Obette, Annie Cheung, Edna Lochner, Joann Larson, Shelva Calhoun, Howard Miller, Jon and Margaret Scott, Robert Perry, Miles Zinn, Marti Howard, Vitalis Ochieng, Julius, Gabriel, Bernadino, Augusta, and of course to editors Wes Eby and Aimee Curtis.

Blessings on the Wairaka Nazarene church in Uganda for their wonderful reception of our family.

Thank you to Dr. Mike and Julie VanZant, Dr. Leah Marungu, Dr. Daryll and Verna Stanton, and Phillip Friday for gracious hospitality while at Africa Nazarene University.

Special appreciation to Rob Gailey for the welcome in Mozambique and leopard stalking in Kruger (good thing we had a great driver whose heart finally said yes). Twang!

Siyabonga kakhulu to Hank, my husband and friend, for 25-plus years of loving Africa with me.

To the lover of my soul, Jesus—to You I devote all.

statement on HIV/AIDS

HIV is the *h*uman *i*mmunodeficiency *v*irus, which attacks and gradually destroys the immune system. It leads to a variety of symptoms and opportunistic diseases that are defined as AIDS, or the *a*cquired *i*mmune *d*eficiency *s*yndrome. These diseases are typically tuberculosis, chronic diarrhea, pneumonia, or other respiratory infections, but they can be any disease since the individual has increased vulnerability to illness. AIDS is the leading cause of death worldwide for people ages 15–59.[1]

In Africa AIDS is often referred to as *silumu* ("slim") for the primary visible symptom of loss of weight. Other African slang terms for it include: banana weevil (since a banana weevil eats its fruit from the inside out), broom or sweeper (the virus sweeps through and decimates entire villages), or jackfruit (a metaphor for the noxious-smelling, sticky fruit of the tropics).

Whatever the name, HIV is transmitted through four major paths: unprotected sexual contact, contaminated needles or razor blades, blood transfusions, or mother-to-child transmissions before, during, or after birth.

AIDS symptoms develop an average of 8 to 10 years after infection if the person was previously healthy. When HIV/AIDS has infected five percent of a country's adult population, it becomes an epidemic.

PROLOGUE
soul cry

"The Soul, which is spirit, cannot dwell in dust; it is carried along to dwell in the blood" (Augustine).

"As a girl I rarely saw a coffin. When people died, they were measured for one. Now coffins are sold next to living room furniture" (Rev. Elizabeth Musimbi, NCM East Africa Coordinator).

✳ ✳ ✳

At the end of 2004 a massive 9.0 earthquake 6 miles under the Indian Ocean stunned the world. The quake shifted 620 miles of a geological plate and disturbed the

A coffin in an African furniture store

earth's rotation, unleashing gigantic tsunami waves that traveled 500 miles per hour and reached 33 feet high. The tsunami wiped out entire villages and killed more than 287,000 people in 11 countries.

The best way to describe the AIDS crisis in Africa and around the world is to liken it to a tsunami. It is a disease of the blood, traveling faster than experts ever dreamed, outpacing medical projections more than three-fold. Perhaps scariest of all is that AIDS is not reaching a natural limit in several countries like Zimbabwe, Swaziland, and Botswana. Able to mutate its shape to avoid detection, it has evolved into at least 10 new strains, complicating the search for a cure. AIDS is also increasing in every world region, obliterating families and communities to the tune of 240,000 deaths and 420,000 new infections every month. Every month! It is hard to wrap our minds around such astonishing numbers.

Sadly, sub-Saharan Africa stands at the epicenter of the "AIDS tsunami." With just 10 percent of the world's population, it has 70 percent of the world's AIDS patients. People may have different ideas of Africa, but to me this giant continent is simply *home.* No matter where I am, Africa seeps in like sand from the desert. I find myself drawn and compelled by a deep sense of connection to the places and the people. As a missionary kid in Swaziland, I fell in love with this small beautiful country of a million people known as "the Switzerland of Africa." The Swazis are my family, a warm and gracious people.

Many years ago one of the first Nazarene missionaries to Africa, Harmon Schmelzenbach, gave a stirring plea: "The lost and dying in Swaziland are crying in the night." Today you can still hear their soul's cry: Swaziland has the unenviable status of having the highest prevalence rate of HIV/AIDS in the world, a staggering 42.6 percent. In 1995 Swazis had a life expectancy of 61 years; by 2010 their average life expectancy is predicted to be just 27.[2] The Swazis are at risk of losing their culture, heritage, and future.

But not just Swaziland. AIDS is the leading cause of death in sub-Saharan Africa. It kills more people than all the wars, famines, natural disasters, and all other diseases combined.[3] Over a two-year span I traveled to Africa three times to do research for this book. I spoke with a variety of people from 18 African countries: truck drivers, shop workers, nurses, pastors, orphans, the unemployed, volunteers, grandmothers, and church leaders. I came away with one unshakeable conclusion: The Church has the only solution for the AIDS crisis in Africa.

AIDS is a painful tragedy and, yes, these pages contain some grim statistics and heartbreaking stories. But ultimately this is a book about hope. It tells the stories of heroes, of God's powerful grace, of courage in the darkest valleys, of the soul hope the Church is providing. Join me on the journey.

Ellen Decker

one
SOUL
BETRAYAL

"The soul never thinks without a picture"
(Aristotle).

A lengthy commercial truck route stretches from Malawi to Zimbabwe. Along a desolate section of this road women have set up temporary shelters in the hopes of earning some money or food in exchange for sex.

A truck driver named Paul in Mozambique was blunt about it. "They have sex to eat. Most of them have children and no man and no job. They have to eat." I asked him about AIDS. His reply startled me. On a continent where every country was at one time colonialized, to many Africans the AIDS acronym stands for "Americans Idea to Destroy Sex." The dismal AIDS statistics are viewed as "a way to scare black people into making less babies." When I asked Paul if truck drivers use condoms, he laughed. "How can you eat a candy with the wrapper on?"

The average price a woman earns when she risks her life on that lonely stretch of road? Less than $5.

✳ ✳ ✳

The HIV/AIDS epidemic is roaring through Africa like a massive tidal wave, unlike any plague the world has ever seen. It is bigger, infecting more than 30 million Africans who will most likely die from it this decade. It is crueler, lingering, hiding in people for years before they wither and die painfully, in the meanwhile spreading to others. It is ruthless, inflicting economic devastation by killing off the most productive people in Africa, the parents of young children and the primary wage earners.

Conversations like the one I had with Paul are important because they show the complexity of the AIDS crisis that the church is facing. While in North America the spread of the virus is primarily limited to small subgroups of homosexuals and drug-users, the factors that contribute to the crisis in the African heterosexual community are multifaceted and difficult to overcome. As an illness, AIDS is aggravated by many factors including poverty, tribal customs, status of women, lack of education, abusive behaviors, prostitution, civil wars, and mobile labor forces. The results across Africa are nothing less than tragic.

Nations are losing their best and brightest. In Botswana a 15-year-old boy has an 85 percent chance of dying from AIDS. In Zambia the life expectancy has already plummeted to a mere 32 years (compare this to a worldwide average of 67 years in 2000).[4] The death odometer from HIV/AIDS at the end of 2004 was 8,000 a day and accelerating. That is the equivalent of 20 jumbo jets full of people crashing—every single day. It is a disease of mass destruction! In South Africa alone, the adult death rate doubled from 1998 to 2003, and deaths among women aged 20-49 skyrocketed by 168 percent.[5]

The elderly in Africa, with no retirement benefits, have traditionally relied on their working sons or daughters to care for them; today those children are sick and dying. This not only leaves old people without support, it saddles them with debt from funeral costs and child-rearing expenses. Several nations in Africa are seeing their gross domestic product numbers dip alarmingly, threatening the future economic development in countries where the quality of life is already spiraling downward.

The number of AIDS orphans is exploding. Already there are 14 million in sub-Saharan Africa; one out of every five children in Swaziland is an orphan.[6] Sadly, orphans are at great risk for malnutrition, abuse, sexual exploitation, and contracting AIDS. Nazarene pastors are overwhelmed with caring for orphans and caregivers.

Almost without exception, every pastor I spoke with in 18 African countries had taken AIDS orphans into their families and homes. Some had more than 10, and two families had more than 20. For most of them, this strains an already tight budget. Pastor Menya in Uganda had 4 children follow him home after he conducted their mother's funeral. They had no other place to go.

Educational systems are in crisis. One million African schoolchildren lost their teachers to HIV/AIDS in 2004.[7] Nazarene churches are scrambling for creative ways to educate orphans. In the Democratic Republic of the Congo (DRC), where many orphans are also traumatized from the country's long civil war, Katindo Church of the Nazarene saw the urgent needs. They collected money, food, and clothes and even paid school fees. Other churches chipped in; 65 orphans are being supported. This in a country where the average annual income is just $100![8] Pastor Ushindi stated, "It is the desire of the church to enable these children to overcome the ordeal of war and AIDS and to grow in their Christian faith."

When I visited Livingstone, Zambia, I was amazed at the efforts of a local Nazarene church to educate 100 AIDS orphans. They had one room with broken windows. Black paint on the wall was the "blackboard." They had no books, no paper, and no writing utensils. They simply had four volunteer teachers and a determination to help the community orphans.

Health systems are overwhelmed. In African countries where the government may have only $2-$5 per patient per year for health care, the costs of treating AIDS patients are staggering to their economy. Even the $6 HIV blood test is beyond the average person's reach. Additionally, because HIV is an assault on the immune system, a patient usually develops a series of illnesses before dying: tuberculosis, pneumonia, meningitis, or diarrhea, all increasing medical costs and straining limited personnel.

Dr. Samuel Hynd, retired 80-year-old Nazarene medical missionary in Swaziland, was still working 40-60 hours each week at a health clinic in Manzini in 2005. His daughter Audrey shared with me, "There are days when dad is really tired and he wants to rest. Then he sees the line of HIV/AIDS patients, many who waited all day or even overnight, and he knows he must continue on."

Hunger is on the increase. Even without AIDS, life in Africa is a constant effort to tilt in one's favor the fragile balance between survival and extinction. One of the tragic ironies is that while nutrition plays a key role in the longevity of the HIV-infected person, food is harder to come by. As surely as drought, as quickly as locusts, AIDS is devouring the continent's cash crops as farmers fall ill and wives and children must spend more of their time caring for them rather than tilling the land.

At the same time, Africa was the only world region between 1990 and 2000 that saw an *increase* in the number of people who live on less than $1 per day.[9] Families desperate for an AIDS cure will sell their most valuable items, or animals previously used as a source of milk or eggs to pay for treatment.

Losing the next generation. Sub-Saharan Africa is the only region in the world to have more women than men infected with HIV, which means more women are dying or becoming infertile. Perhaps one of the greatest tragedies about AIDS in Africa is that just two doses of medicine costing $7 can help prevent the transmission from mother to child—yet most cannot afford it.

Many mothers pass on the infection through breastfeeding. Nazarene nurse Lucia Thomas said, "South African culture demands a mother breast-feed. We give free milk at the hospital, but many are scared to use it because of the stigma. I recommend that HIV mothers take pills to dry up their milk, otherwise the temptation may become too great. On the other hand, I have seen babies who tested negative for HIV die from diarrhea because of lack of clean water for bottle-feeding. There are no easy answers."

AIDS weakens national and global security. Nazarene nurse Mary Magagula shares about visiting a clinic in Swaziland where many women had opportunistic infections. She soon discovered that women were being enticed by a tin of fish or a packet of beans to sleep with the soldiers in the barracks down the road. Drought and hunger even caused some husbands to encourage it. "People are hungry," Mary shared. "When there is nothing, they will do anything to get food. One woman had three children; the father was gone. She doesn't like what she is doing. None of them like it. But they want to feed their kids." As soldiers get sick, they are less able to defend their nation, maintain order, or participate in peacekeeping roles.

Businesses that rely on personnel are also feeling the pinch as more workers fall ill; education and training programs cannot keep up. As we move toward increased globalization, the free world has a vested interest in a stable and democratic Africa. Not convinced? Just look at

Mary Magagula

your clothing labels. Many shirts sold at Wal-Mart are made in Lesotho, where almost one-third of the population is now HIV positive.

* * *

A proverb from Burundi says, "It is easy to pull a thorn out of someone else's skin." How easy it is for us to judge another person's situation, using it as an excuse to not care or be involved, forgetting that we are all saved by grace. Even though we know that the spread of AIDS is largely behavior-based, it is not easy to stop an epidemic that so betrays the soul.

two
SOUL
SEARCHING

"Put your ear down close to your soul and listen hard" (Anne Sexton).

Imagine this is your life: You wake up in the morning and are horrified to discover your infant died during the night. Your husband works 300 miles away, comes home twice a year, and sleeps around in between. When your best friend asked her husband to use a condom, she was beaten and thrown on the streets. Next door a teenage girl is struggling to raise four younger siblings with no source of income.

Begrudgingly, you continue going to work where every third coworker is HIV positive. In the cafeteria you hear a rumor about a woman who admitted she had the scourge and neighbors stoned her to death. With your monthly income of $25, you know if you get AIDS your only choice will be 80 cents per day for medicine or food for your family. You go to bed wondering if you will reach 35. On Saturdays you attend funerals, one of which is your own child's.

❊   ❊   ❊

Petua Aliba is a 28-year-old Nazarene widow in Uganda. Her husband died of AIDS when she was seven

Petua Aliba and her children

months pregnant with her second child. "I married right out of high school," Petua shared. "I had no idea he was already HIV positive. I was very angry for a long time, but when I became a Christian two years ago, Jesus helped me to forgive."

Petua, who now has AIDS herself, worries what will happen to her two sons, Jackson and James. Her family wants her to go to a witch doctor and marry another man to support her and the children. "When I feel sick I can't provide for my children. Yet I am a Christian. I will not go to the witch doctor, and I will not spread AIDS.

Somehow Jesus will help me." Three weeks later Petua was evicted from her home for not having her rent: $27.

When I spoke with Sarah Noel in Tanzania, her husband had been dead just three weeks. "God is giving me strength to deal with my husband's death," she commented. "I have a wonderful HIV support group. We pray for each other. We know we are infected, and we accept it. But our biggest concern remains: What is going to happen to our children?"

Across Africa, women like Petua and Sarah are bearing the brunt of the plague. Several studies have shown that 7 out of 10 women in Africa with AIDS are innocent victims. Yet less than 10 percent of pregnant women are being offered services to prevent transmission of HIV to their infants.[10] The cultural treatment of women has a huge impact on the spread of AIDS in Africa.

Global AIDS Day on December 1, 2004, was dedicated to improving protection for women and girls. While women are expected to be modest and submissive, male sexual entitlement has strong social and cultural support in most African countries. Women who have unequal status in society may submit to a man's sexual demands because she feels she has no choice or is afraid of being beaten.

When I was 17, my parents were offered the generous price of 75 cows for my hand in marriage in Siteki, Swaziland (they turned it down). This practice of *lobola* (bride price) is common across southern Africa. Men then believe they have the right to act as they please, which includes sleeping around. The woman's responsibility is to stay at home, cook, clean, take care of the children, and be available for her husband. Additionally, if the wife does not produce children, the husband has the right to demand his money back (even though it may be the man who gave his wife a sexually transmitted disease that made her infertile). If a woman chooses to leave her husband, she is a disgrace to her family. Since culture dictates that children belong to the father, a woman can lose her children as well.

Because children are so highly prized in many African cultures, young girls are often pressured to bear a child even before marriage as proof of fertility. Other cultural practices that increase the risk of HIV infection are polygamy and child marriage. In some cultures, when a girl begins menstruating she must sleep with the village chief, or have sex with an arranged stranger as preparation for adulthood.

In Malawi a custom called *kulowa kufa* dictates a grieving widow must sleep with someone in the village chosen by the elders. If she refuses, they believe other family members will die. "There are still chiefs who do not believe in AIDS," said Mwabi Mwanza, Nazarene Compassionate Ministries coordinator for Malawi. "In the Chewa and Yao tribes young girls are taken far from the village to sleep with men to be cleansed."

Economic inequality aggravates matters. The burden for caring for sick relatives typically falls on the woman.

Ellen Decker and Mwabi Mwanza

If a wife's husband dies, often leaving her infected, his relatives may take her husband's property and leave her penniless. She may then resort to selling her body to survive and perpetuate the vicious cycle.

For males, it is a cultural expectation in many African countries to prove manhood by having sex by age 15. It is often a false sense of male ego that prompts many men to refuse testing for AIDS, even when they fall ill. Many African men have felt disempowered by a history of colonialism, racism, and poverty. They are reluctant to give up their hold over women. Only Christ's transforming power can help men understand the moral mandate to respect the dignity of each person.

For women who have been abused and mistreated, the Church has the good news that in Christ "there is neither male nor female" (Gal. 3:28). Women have equal worth. As Christ's church, we can combat the second-class status of women.

A Kiganda proverb states, "If you educate a woman, you have educated a population." NCM Africa is in the process of training 400 Nazarene women leaders. Training includes biblical principles on sexuality, the positives and negatives of local culture, gender issues and discrimination, sex education, productivity and food security, and ways of empowering women to protect themselves against sexual violence. Each group of women then completes a workable plan for training and education of women in their home countries.

✻　✻　✻

Think for a moment: one out of every five Nazarenes is from the continent of Africa. Almost every Nazarene on the Africa Region has been somehow affected by the HIV/AIDS tragedy. This means many of our brothers and sisters are dying, grieving, or caring for survivors. Most of us have lived protected by two oceans from the rest of the world far too long. Just as the tsunami in Southeast Asia brought the stark reality of their living conditions into our living room, the AIDS crisis is confronting our Christian worldview. Just who is our neighbor?

> Almost every Nazarene on the Africa Region has been somehow affected by the HIV/AIDS tragedy.

AIDS is the greatest challenge the worldwide church faces today. If we search our souls for what God desires, we will discover that we are uniquely poised to respond to the behavioral influences that are spreading AIDS. We have the wonderful holiness message that embraces abstinence before marriage and faithfulness in marriage. We have the leadership, the incredible infrastructure for training, and the compassion for the sick, the orphans, and the caregivers.

The Church of the Nazarene reaches into communities and homes across Africa with trusted moral authority. Only Christianity can approach AIDS with hope. We offer the best and most affordable medicine—a Savior who redeems us, loves us, and offers eternal life.

three
SOUL
SALVATION

"It is not proper to cure the body without the soul" (Loomis).

Dawn in Africa is never pale; the sun catapults from the horizon like a peeled apricot. Up at 5:30 A.M. on a Saturday, I am leaving Maputo, Mozambique. We pass through incredible vistas of poverty and rubbish along a road of gigantic potholes. Already the sun is shimmering in its own heat.

I blink. Surely what I think I am seeing is just a mirage.

There is a massive graveyard that stretches on, football field after football field, and still it goes on. Even at this time of day, there are already a thousand or more people clustered around dozens and dozens of graves. This is the first wave of the day's funerals, cycled through quickly to bury hundreds, thousands, before nightfall. Tears wash across my cheeks. Soundlessly, my lungs search for a word to speak. I want to hold the world responsible.

We drive on in silence into the searing white heat of the sun.

❋   ❋   ❋

When I visited Maputo Central, the largest Nazarene congregation in Africa, they were just beginning their AIDS ministry at the end of 2003. I met with senior pastor Bessie Tsambe, associate pastor Assa Suéia, and their prayer group. Surprisingly, their prayer group for AIDS consisted of five young men, committed to praying weekly for HIV/AIDS in their country. When asked why they were so passionate about it, they replied, "Because it is most affecting young males just like us. If it weren't for God's grace in our lives, we also could be dying and hopeless."

I then traveled rutted dirt roads to Luís Cabral to visit an AIDS volunteer group. The group, led by Sidália Chongo of World Relief, was made up of ladies from 34 denominations that volunteer as caregivers to AIDS patients in their communities. They meet together once a month to pray, to encourage each other, and for training. Their group's name is *Tshembeka*, which means "Be Faithful."

One lady shared through streaming tears that she visited an AIDS patient for the first time and made plans to return later, but the patient died. This precious lady felt intense grief, sobbing, "I never would have left without telling her about Jesus if I'd known she was going to die."

Amazingly, some Christians are hesitant to help because AIDS often comes from immoral sex. They seem to forget that the role of the Church is to do all we can to prevent people from going to hell. Rev. Charles Spurgeon (1834-1892) wrote: "If sinners be damned, at least let them leap to hell over our bodies. If they will perish, let them perish with our arms about their knees. Let no one go there unwarned and unprayed for."

There are so many living in darkness. On a road I traveled near Kisumu, Kenya, a billboard reads, "AIDS is not witchcraft. AIDS is real."

"There are still people who believe that the disease is an attack from evil ancestor spirits," Pastor David Malinzi in Uganda told me. "Many people here think having AIDS means an enemy has bewitched them," shared Rev. Wellington Obotte, missionary to Tanzania, "and only a witch doctor has an antidote."

Traditional healers take advantage of people's fears, charging exorbitant prices to burn incense or rub ashes on a wound. Some traditional healers themselves are spreading AIDS by using an unclean knife to give a patient "elevenses," two vertical cuts "to let the evil spirits escape" their body. In some cultures a witch doctor has girls serving him as slaves, or he performs fertility ceremonies by having sexual intercourse with the women.

The Nazarene church in Africa is responding to this spiritual darkness with a clear call to holiness living. Rev. Daniel Mokebe, Africa Central Field director, said at the Africa Regional Conference in November 2003, "What are some of the methods that help us fulfill the Great Commission in Africa? NCM has done a great work in recent years . . . through conducting training sessions for AIDS awareness and training local churches."

Zambia

Zambia declared an emergency in September 2004, stating that one out of five Zambians was infected with HIV. In this country of 10 million people, 75 percent of families have taken in at least one AIDS orphan.[11]

NCM has trained more than 25,000 pastors, church lay leaders, and community members across Zambia. Rev. Gilbert Bakasa, Zambia NCM coordinator, began an AIDS ministry in every Nazarene church in Zambia. In fact, it is now their policy that every new preaching point also begins an AIDS ministry.

Every church has developed a team of volunteers to visit the sick, pray for them, and lead people to Christ. The NCM Zambia ministry statement reads in part, "In

(l to r): NCM coordinators, Célestin Chishibanji, DRC, and Gilbert Bakasa, Zambia

AIDS ministry we don't mind the condition of someone's sickness. Our goal is to love them, care for them, and preach Jesus to them before they die of AIDS. We believe that Jesus, our Hope, provides salvation even in the last minute of life to all who believe."

"The gospel cannot be left behind in our counseling with AIDS patients," said Mike Lilema, Sunday School superintendent of Kaunda Square Nazarene. "We have to talk about the unconditional love of God, His forgiveness of sin, the hope there is in Jesus. The gospel is life."

Churches across Zambia are collecting clothes, blankets, food, and materials for widows and orphans. Volunteers are helping elderly caregivers with odd jobs, and churches take offerings for AIDS patients, caregivers, and orphans. Currently 140 churches in Zambia are supporting a whopping 6,000 orphans and 1,571 caregivers. This is phenomenal in a country where the majority live on less than $1 per day. Truly, Nazarenes in Zambia have caught the vision of "compassion as a lifestyle"!

Every 10 seconds one person dies from HIV/AIDS and two are infected.

And they are passing on their vision to the next generation. After one Youth Week of fellowship and training on AIDS, Zambian youth put their love into action. Taking brooms, hoes, and cleaning detergents to a local hospital, they scrubbed and cleaned and hoed and raked. They visited the sick and the dying, encouraging and praying with patients.

✻ ✻ ✻

Not just in Zambia, but all across Africa, the Church of the Nazarene is blessing thousands, many of whom we will now meet in heaven:

- "In the past I used to drink alcohol and practice prostitution, and now I have AIDS," shared a viewer of the *JESUS* film in Kenya. "That evening when I heard the Word of God and accepted it, I truly believed in Him."

- In Ethiopia a devout Muslim demanded to know why NCM would help AIDS orphans. When he heard why, he prayed to receive Christ that day.

- "As we did door-to-door evangelism, we met a boy named John whose parents had died because of AIDS," a *JESUS* film team in Tanzania shared. "When we shared with him about the love of God and how sin separates us from God, he began crying. He told us that he had been thinking about abandoning his five younger siblings. We prayed with him, and he gave his life to Christ."

- Rev. Pato of the Sitsatsaweni Nazarene Church in Swaziland led Mr. Dlomo, a 38-year-old AIDS patient, to the Lord. Dlomo's inspiring testimonies to colleagues led others to Christ. At Dlomo's funeral his brother became a Christian, and so it continues.

✻ ✻ ✻

A small part of the Maputo graveyard

D. Park

A Togolese proverb states, "The tears running down your face do not blind you." The day I drove by the Maputo graveyard, I saw with startling clarity the urgency to reach AIDS patients with the gospel. The reality is that every 10 seconds one person dies from HIV/AIDS and two are infected. The devastating personal, societal, and political consequences of this disease are escalating every day.

The United Nations estimates that Africa will have 89 million new cases of HIV/AIDS within the next two decades.[12] They even admitted on July 14, 2004, that churches are crucial in the global effort against HIV/AIDS. For Christians, that mandate is even more pressing: soul salvation is at stake.

four
SOUL
SOLUTION

"The soul of man is larger than the sky. It is deeper than the ocean or the abysmal dark of the unfathomed center" (Hartley Coleridge).

They say you never forget the smells and textures of your youth. Climbing leadwood trees. Exploring green hills and cool riverbeds. The hazy yellow warmth of bright mornings. Goats braying and chickens fussing. Today I am visiting Raleigh Fitkin Memorial Hospital in Manzini, Swaziland, where my sister Sharon was born over 30 years ago. I find it is very different from my memories of running through the halls as a carefree child. Everything needs paint. Broken metal beds with thin mattresses line up in rows, robbing patients of privacy. Flies buzz, and an oppressive heat rolls in from the open windows.

I stop by a bed, drawn to it when I hear its occupant is the same age as my son Jason, but I do not see any similarities in this 16-year-old boy afflicted with AIDS. How ironic that just a few years ago his "rite to manhood," circumcision with an HIV-bloodied blade, became his passage to an early death. His arms are so thin the elbows look like protruding bones. His neck and face are covered with sores. His shallow breathing turns his ill blood over and over. I empty my pockets, knowing I can never give enough. Maybe he will buy a cold drink, or perhaps some aspirin to ease the pain.

He stares at me, and in his frightened eyes I see the wish to still live.

❊ ❊ ❊

Swaziland made great strides in education, health care, and personal income until the late 1990s when AIDS began to strike down the middle generation. In 1992 its HIV rate was only 3.9 percent; its current rate of 42.6 percent has been called "a national extermination

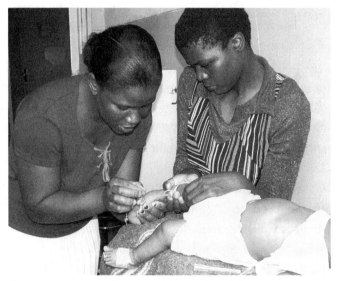

Swazi nurses care for an infant with AIDS.

notice." A decade of too little rain has added to the country's misery, decimating the maize and cotton crops.

Today two-thirds of Swazis live in unbelievable poverty: just 45 cents per day. Unemployment averages 40 percent.[13] Problems overwhelm the medical system, including increased patient load and staff illness. More time is needed to attend funerals. AIDS threatens the army, police, and teachers, all critical to a nation functioning well.

> A 15-year-old in Swaziland today has a mere 20 percent chance of reaching 35 years old. Twenty percent!

Poverty, hunger, and disease are all increasing. The death rate doubled in a seven-year period at the turn of the century. A 15-year-old in Swaziland today has a mere 20 percent chance of reaching 35 years old. Twenty percent! Families are stretched beyond the breaking point as they care for sick members. If a person falls ill, the family kills a chicken for extra nourishment. The potential of eggs and future chickens is destroyed. As the illness is protracted, and the loss of income mounts, the social fabric of the family tears irreparably.

Already there are more than 15,000 households in Swaziland headed by orphaned children. Each of these has approximately four children with an average age of just 11.[14]

"We are seeing children heading more and more households," said Marjorie Mavuso, a Nazarene who is the coordinator for monitoring and evaluation for the Swaziland government's National Emergency Response Committee on HIV/AIDS. "Not that parents didn't die before AIDS, but the social structure in Swaziland did not allow a child to stay alone. Now there are increasingly no relatives. One day we will wake up and find we don't have a Swaziland. By that I mean if the people who are to raise a child in the Swazi tradition are dying, it means we are losing a way of life, a culture, an identity. And if we don't have that identity, Swaziland will be gone."

When King Mswati III declared AIDS a national disaster in 1999, the government included the role of the church in its strategy to combat AIDS. Swaziland has four political districts with a total of 55 *tinkundlas* (constituencies). Every *tinkundla* has an HIV committee, and every committee a pastor. There are over 130 Nazarene churches in Swaziland, also divided into four districts.

"God gave the church authority," Marjorie explained. "We can bring solutions to this issue through the message of holiness."

Rev. Cariot Shongwe, superintendent of Swaziland Central District, agrees that the church must lead by example. "So many charitable organizations use their money for offices and supplies and fancy business cards," he told me. "I strongly disagree with that. Our money is used for food for the orphans; it goes for medicines and pain relief for the dying. It's time for the people of Christ to respond like Jesus did!"

B. Dawson

Soup kitchen for orphans in Manzini

From this passion the Central District HIV/AIDS Task Force was formed. Retired nurse Mary Magagula had hoped to have some time to relax and enjoy her grandchildren. "Instead," she shared, "I thought of all the people out there suffering from AIDS who really needed someone to care." Mary is the coordinator of the task force, whose massive challenge is to find solutions for home-based care for AIDS patients; health education for schools, churches, and communities; and support for the destitute and orphaned.

Each volunteer member of the task force pays dues to help support the program. They believe the Swazi proverb, "Without effort no harvest will be abundant."

The task force has also started a soup kitchen for orphans in Manzini and has trained 80 care supporters. The volunteers go into homesteads, taking medicine, vitamins, food, and clothing. They are the unsung heroes: holding hands, stroking heads, touching blistered skin, cooling parched lips.

Some, like Clarah Gamedze and Ethel Dlamini, are appointed by the Swazi Chief's councils *(tinkundlas)*. Others, like Dinah Zwane, simply volunteer, often giving their own food and clothes. They even wash corpses, using gloves, to help the grieving families. They minister to people who are hungry, destitute, and in pain with no one to care for them.

One is 17-year-old Phetsile who suffers from epilepsy. At 15 she was stabbed and raped (a false, terrible lie spreading across Africa is that having sex with a virgin will cure AIDS). Instead of looking forward to high school graduation, she is now dealing with AIDS and trying to raise a toddler.

Another family's fourth child was stillborn. Their 2-year-old died next, followed shortly by the mother. The mother-in-law came to help, but soon both she and her son died, leaving behind two kids, 8 and 11.

Similar stories can be repeated thousands upon thousands of times across Swaziland and sub-Saharan Africa. However, thanks to caring Swazi Nazarenes, these children became Christians and have hope for a future. Care supporters, particularly Evelyn Shongwe, have led many to Christ.

Nevertheless, it is a heartbreaking ministry. In one year the task force received 471 new patients; 114 died. The church is facing a major loss of members at the same time masses of orphans need to be cared for. Swaziland is mountainous, and homesteads are scattered. Transportation is a huge challenge. Stigma is still an obstacle, even in churches. One educated Christian had to seek employment (along with 51,000 others every year) outside of Swaziland. While away from his wife for months on end, he fell into sexual temptation. To his death he insisted he was poisoned rather than admitting he had AIDS.

Though the darkness looms, solutions that Nazarenes are providing across Africa are glimmers of light. The care-supporter approach used by the Central District is so successful that other denominations across Swaziland and in surrounding countries are asking to be trained in this strategy.

The morning Mary Magagula and I visited an AIDS hospice, a woman died from AIDS. When I expressed sorrow, Mary's response was profound: "We are a people of hope. We put our heart and soul into helping those with AIDS. But we never give up hoping that someday God will give us the ultimate solution to AIDS."

five
SOUL
SUPPORT

"The soul is known by its acts" (Thomas Aquinas).

When she heard she had AIDS, Annette thought she would drop dead right then. Instead, she found new purpose. Now 36, Annette has lived with AIDS for 10 years. Coughing frequently into her handkerchief as we talked, Annette credits her church for supporting and encouraging her. Besides coordinating her church's visitation, Annette visits five people every day, sharing her faith and hope with them. While she wonders what will happen to her four teens, especially the youngest who is frequently sick, Annette radiates a positive attitude. When asked if she would like to say something to the worldwide church, she responded, "I would encourage everyone to love and comfort the sick in their communities."

❋ ❋ ❋

In their official stance on AIDS, Nazarene Compassionate Ministries, cooperating through the World Mission Department of the church, resolves to:

- Inform and educate Nazarenes on the issues of the HIV/AIDS pandemic

Annette

- Teach scriptural principles of purity before marriage, faithfulness within marriage, and avoidance of risky behavior
- Empower the global church, in partnership with other faith-based agencies, to develop programs of care for the infected and affected, without discrimination to any.

NCM believes it is critical to provide support to those on the front lines of the AIDS crisis through prayer, training, and raising awareness. Exodus 18:21 says, "Select capable men from among all the people—men who fear God, trustworthy men who hate dishonest gain—and appoint them as officials over thousands, hundreds, fifties, and tens." The church in Africa is struggling with a higher percentage of widows and orphans, an increase in members' deaths, and the blow of economic devastation. Yet it is valiantly equipping capable pastors and laypeople to support the sick, the caregivers, and the orphans.

Rev. Trino Jara, NCM-Africa coordinator, has traveled across the African continent presenting workshops on AIDS, some in conjunction with Nazarene Youth International (NYI) and Rev. Monte Cyr, Global NYI president. Their goal is for at least two people from each of the 111 African districts to receive HIV/AIDS training and to hold AIDS awareness workshops at every youth camp.

Monte described one of the AIDS training events. "After eight hours on roads, some of them dirt, and crossing two rivers, we arrived at the Salamba Church of the Nazarene in the small village of Kucha, Ethiopia. We were met by about 100 people from three zones on the district who expressed such an incredible hunger for spiritual teaching and leadership training. Many walked for miles just to attend. They had to slog through mud, sleep on the ground, and stack themselves almost on top of each other in mud huts when it rained, yet no complaints. Only gratefulness to participate and learn."

Youth leaders from across northern Mozambique eagerly soaked in the hands-on tools and techniques at their workshop. "All around them young people are dying physically and spiritually," Monte shared. "They know what is at stake, and they threw themselves into the training."

Sixty youth leaders in Zimbabwe took a three-day training seminar that included biblical training and HIV/AIDS ministry. Two Nigerian pastors shared their training at two district conventions and many of their 43 churches. Several prevention workshops were held in Abidjan, Côte d'Ivoire.

The church in Benin, a country whose HIV rate jumped from one to seven percent in just five years, hosted an AIDS conference. The speaker was from the *Mercy Ship Anastasis,* which does AIDS seminars wherever they dock. Many of the non-Nazarene attendees expressed appreciation to the Church of the Nazarene for dealing with the issue.

After training leaders in the northern part of South Africa, 28 churches caught the vision and implemented agricultural projects to support caregivers and orphans.

A group of mothers bought a package of new razor blades to prevent HIV for 30 young men who were being circumcised in their village.

In the Democratic Republic of the Congo (DRC), two churches have begun a joint clinic that tests and educates people in their communities about HIV/AIDS. Each month they have a special campaign that emphasizes prevention and behavior change. In Goma a team of Nazarenes visits the sick in hospitals and prisons.

In East Africa, NCM coordinator Rev. Elizabeth

Musimbi stresses self-reliance. "There are lots of resources in Africa," says Elizabeth. "For instance, the sisal plant can be made into baskets, ropes, and mats. The Kiatine church saw the potential but lacked the thread. NCM provided the thread, and now they are making items to support their AIDS ministries." Elizabeth also counsels patients to make wills and provide for their families.

In Uganda pastors support the sick through regular counseling and meeting basic physical needs. "Pastors are not blaming the sick," shared Pastor David Malinzi. "Instead they take every opportunity to introduce them to Jesus." Initially hesitant to discuss AIDS, churches now are encouraging people with AIDS to share their testimonies. AIDS lessons are taught through songs, dramas, stories, and Bible lessons. Initiatives to support 896 orphans and 187 Christian caregivers include used clothing drives, counseling, vegetable gardens, a fish pond, and compassionate teams that visit the sick to pray and give them soup, salt, and sugar. Kirugu Church of the Nazarene with Pastor Sarah Nalongo has a building and a retired nurse; their vision is to begin a clinic if they can get the funds for medicines.

In Benin the HIV rate jumped from one to seven percent in just five years.

Malawi

Malawi began community-based care training programs in 2004. Training is helping hundreds of communities to confront myths and taboos as well as break barriers of rejection, stigmatization, and isolation that many of them had been imposing on those infected with AIDS.

In the capitals of Mzuzu and Lilongwe, prostitution is high. Truckers drive to the Lilongwe Hotel where girls as young as 12 flash open their coats to entice them in. At convention centers across Malawi, names of prostitutes are handed out. Girls who date government ministers receive special privileges. "When their impoverished backgrounds only allow a bowl of porridge a day," Mwabi Mwanza shared, "the temptation is great."

In Mzuzu, six village heads attended the NCM training; several expressed delight that the church encourages abstinence. The Mzuzu church also showed the *JESUS* film. When attendees saw the prostitute, they began weeping. They were overwhelmed that Jesus loved the woman and treated her well in spite of her sin. While AIDS is a tragedy for millions of families, it is also a tremendous opportunity for the church to love and evangelize them.

A Personal Story

Lucia Thomas, a Nazarene nurse in South Africa, remembers her first AIDS patient in 1988. "I mostly ignored him," she admits. "When I had to give him medication, I gave it to him in a disposable cup so I never had to touch him." Eventually the Holy Spirit convicted her, and she asked the man to forgive her. From that day she promised the Lord she would treat HIV persons with the dignity they deserve.

For over 13 years Lucia has worked directly with AIDS patients. She often has the difficult task of informing a new mother she is HIV positive; out of this she has developed a wonderful, caring ministry of counseling. Lucia encourages women to live positively, to eat properly, and to take care of themselves. She counsels them about their rights under the law and their human dignity.

Tragedy struck home when Lucia's brother was diagnosed with HIV in 2003. "I've counseled hundreds of affected people over the years," she acknowledges, "but when it comes home . . . it's much worse. It's not as easy as you think . . . it's very difficult. You really learn to lean on Jesus as your soul support and realize just how critical that support is for every person affected by HIV/ AIDS."

six
SOUL SURVIVORS

"The one thing in the world of value is the soul" (Ralph Waldo Emerson).

Church let out under the hot African sky in Jinja, Uganda. I sat on a rough-hewn wooden bench, hunched forward so I could hear the soft-spoken voice of Dorcus, an AIDS orphan who lives with elderly grandparents. Eleven years old and in the fifth grade, the only outward indication that Dorcus has AIDS is her wispy hair. She is an intelligent, articulate child who enjoys singing and netball (similar to basketball). Her favorite treat is a cold drink. Science and English are her best subjects, although some days she leaves school early because her energy runs out.

I asked her how she coped when she didn't feel good and could only watch the other children play. Her innocent brown eyes rose to gaze intently at me. "I pray, and Jesus helps me." Like it was the most natural thing in the world.

At the end of our conversation I asked, "If you could ask anything of the global church, what would you ask for?"

Her soft reply shattered my heart: "I would ask them to pray for my pain to go away."

❊ ❊ ❊

Dorcus

Even if an AIDS cure is found tomorrow, orphaned and vulnerable children will be a reality for our lifetime. Almost without exception, children orphaned by AIDS are stigmatized, malnourished, uneducated, and struggle with emotional trauma. Because of this, they are more likely to become HIV-positive themselves (sub-Saharan Africa accounts for more than 85 percent of all children under 15 living with the disease).[15]

Every day 1,800 children under 15 get HIV and 1,400 children under age 15 die of AIDS-related illnesses.[16]

Another shocking fact: less than 10 percent of the children who have been orphaned or made vulnerable by AIDS receive any public support or services.[17] AIDS does far more than kill the parents. It compounds the suffering of the survivors, the innocent children.

Netsai was orphaned by AIDS. At age 13 she quit school to become the primary caregiver to her four younger siblings, then ages 9, 6, 2, and 1. They cannot afford school fees, and many days they have nothing to eat. All five are underdeveloped from malnutrition.

> Every day 1,400 children under age 15 die of AIDS-related illnesses.

"We put corn into a sack for Netsai and her little family," shared Elaine Bumstead, a Canadian Nazarene who oversaw an NCM distribution of corn in Zimbabwe. "We learned, just recently, that Netsai was sick but could not afford clinic fees. As I talked with her, she coughed and scraped at large sores on her legs. When I questioned others who knew Netsai, I learned she was being sexually abused by men in her village. I was both angry and tearful at the same time. Where is the hope for Netsai?"

Pindile's parents also died from AIDS. At 17, Pindile was left with five younger siblings to care for. Unlike Netsai, Pindile has the loving attention of the Avondale Church of the Nazarene in Harare, Zimbabwe. The church pays school fees, purchases uniforms, and gives them a monthly food allowance. Many Sundays the elders of the church counsel Pindile and other children who head households, asking about their ongoing needs. "The Book of James reminds us that taking care of orphans is true religion," shared Pastor Cosmos Mutowa. "Acts of compassion are part of worship."

The loss of a parent permeates every aspect of a child's life: physical security, emotional well-being, intellectual development, and overall health. This is especially critical when viewed in light of the 4-14 window, the age bracket when most people decide to follow Christ. Across Africa, churches are stepping up to help these little souls.

For example, in the DRC Pastor Bugeshi Désiré and his church have organized a breeding program of goats and ducks, planted a garden of maize, and started a primary school with 112 students. (The "school" is tarpaulin sheeting to protect from the hot sun and stones for chairs.) Ngoma Nazarene with Pastor Thomas Hajabakiga cares for 300 orphans; 130 are HIV positive. Kagarama Nazarene with Pastor Aaron Gafupi began vocational classes in 2000, teaching hundreds of orphans valuable skills.

Orphans and Vulnerable Children

The Church of the Nazarene has an incredible orphans and vulnerable children (OVC) ministry in Kisumu, Kenya, directed by Africa Nazarene University (ANU) graduates Samuel Oketch and Daniel Friday. The brilliance of the program is that it enlists volunteers to find child-headed homes in the communities, then involves local churches to come alongside the children. A beautiful result is that most of the caregivers and orphans "adopted" by local churches eventually become Christians.

The OVC program has organized communities and churches to plant vegetable gardens for children. They encourage church members to donate chicks, and NCM helps by putting iron sheets on the coops. Training is given on AIDS, nutrition, business skills (given by Students in Free Enterprise from ANU), and psychosocial needs.

Eunice and Celine, faithful and trained volunteers, feel called to this ministry. Six days a week they serve Nutro Drink (a porridge with special nutrients) to the children at Brinkman Church of the Nazarene. Every

(l. to r.) Eunice and Celine

week they visit homes affected by AIDS, building relationships with the children. I was privileged to go visiting with them one day.

We stopped in to see Rose Achieng'. Rose, 27, has two children: Teddy, 5, and Nellie, 2. Her husband died when Nellie was 4 months old, and Rose is HIV positive. She still feels good and wants to learn how to sew so she can become self-supporting. Rose attends the program's business training. Teddy and Nellie receive Nutro each day.

At Joyce Ongele's home I learned that Luo tradition dictates that when the father dies, a home must be destroyed to "rid it of the evil spirits." Because Joyce is a Christian, she did not destroy her home when her husband died from AIDS, but she worries what will happen to her 11 children when she is gone. Eunice visits weekly, helping Joyce prepare a memory box for her children.

We had to wake up Betta Omondi when we visited her. She is further along in the stages of AIDS and tires easily. She has typhoid and an amoeba that was giving her severe diarrhea. When she has the energy, Betta sells potatoes. For every large bag she sells, she is given three potatoes. Betta's sister was visiting, doing the cooking and watching five young kids, including her own toddler and a six-month-old with measles. Sitting in Betta's tiny, tiny house with a packed dirt floor, surrounded by stark poverty, disease, and human suffering, I wondered where the hope was.

Betta herself told me. She lives within walking distance of Brinkman Church of the Nazarene. "I am loved and welcomed there," she said. "Celine visits me every week and brings me encouragement and hope." Betta is working on a memory box, although all she owns to put in it is one photo of her husband and her memory journal.

Many of the dying have nothing, not even identification documents. In the past, these people were given a stone to hold, which was then given to their child with the assurance, "Your mother held this stone." Yet NCM wants to give orphans something more. A Kenyan proverb says, "Talking with one another is loving one another." Memory journals and boxes provide an opportunity for parents to "talk" to their children even after they are gone. These expressed hopes and dreams are a lasting legacy of love for the children.

Fanual, 17, dropped out of school to take care of his three younger siblings when his parents died from AIDS. Working day labor when jobs are available, Fanual earns about $1 per day to support his family. They are receiving help in the form of school fees for 15-year-old brother Wycleff. Fanual says, "When people ask how my brother is able to attend school, we say: 'God has done something for us.'"

Kenya acquires 1,000 new orphans every week. Estimates are for 50 million orphans in sub-Saharan Africa by 2010. (That is more than *all* the children living west of the Mississippi in the United States.) These are children who leave school to care for dying parents, who all too soon face adult responsibilities, who wish for more than anything to have the warm presence of someone who cares.

God longs to do something for these soul survivors —through us.

"Seek justice, encourage the oppressed. Defend the cause of the fatherless, plead the case of the widow" (Isa. 1:17).

seven
SOUL
CARE

"The soul gives us resilience—an essential quality since we constantly have to rebound from hardship" (Wynton Marsalis).

I stood transfixed in the doorway of an 8' x 8' room with three thin mattresses on the dirt floor. Eleven girls sleep here every night. As appalling as that seems, they fare much better than many orphans who burrow in the ground or sleep under trees. Their caregivers are pastors Mark and Margaret Kibadawo. Mark is also assistant superintendent on the Uganda Central District. Seeing the increasing number of AIDS orphans in their community, the Kibadawos wanted to help but lacked the resources. Regardless, they have taken in 22 AIDS orphans.

I was curious how their own two sons responded to the influx of children. "At first they resented all the orphans," said Margaret, "but then I taught them what the Word of God says." Apparently they got the message: their younger son willingly moved into a wooden lean-to at the back of the parsonage. He happily told me he lives with his "brothers."

During the week, their church uses its modest one-

room structure as a school with overflow under the jacaranda tree outside. People in the church donate pencils, paper, and used clothing in a "mercy box." In the midst of incredible hardship, the Kibadawos are providing soul care for 24 precious children.

✳ ✳ ✳

During a hot, dusty wait at the Ugandan border my son Ryan and his fiancé, Kendra, befriended a little girl, buying her a cold drink. A man came over and explained to us that her parents died from AIDS. She scavenges at the border because she has no one to care for her. He urged us to take her, saying it would be her only opportunity for a good future.

Behind the tragedy of parents dying and 8,000 children orphaned every day lurks another unfolding hard-

Rev. Mark and Margaret Kibadawo

ship. Thousands and thousands of individuals in every country across this vast continent find themselves thrust into the role of caregiver. In fact, many people are afraid to visit AIDS patients—not because of the disease, but because patients may beg them to care for their children after they die. Many caregivers are children themselves; many more are elderly grandparents, aunts and uncles, or overburdened pastors.

Missionary Verna Stanton's ANU class, "Personal, Family, and Community Health," teaches about AIDS and assigns a community outreach project. One place students are going is Mama Margaret's near the campus. Mama Margaret is a caregiver to 30 orphans. Her home is a little three-room building made of cement with a corrugated tin roof. Outside is their kitchen, a small, half-enclosed shed with a wood fire and a couple of pots. They have no toilet facility. Every day the children have to carry five-gallon cans over a mile and purchase water. Sometimes they only have *ugali* (boiled maize flour cooked stiff) to eat, but Margaret loves the children and treats them as her own.

Caregivers are a vital part of the church's solution to the AIDS crisis in Africa. NCM believes that for long-term sustainability, it is better to assist as many caregivers as possible rather than start orphanages. Orphanages require high and permanent operational costs, and children often lose their cultural heritage. The best response to the AIDS epidemic must be locally relevant, locally directed, and capable of being sustained over a long period of time. The NCM caregivers program meets this criteria.

NCM-Africa encourages every local church to identify the needs of caregivers and to mobilize to minister to them. As funds allow, NCM supports caregivers by providing seed and tools for vegetable gardens and training for income-generating activities.

The Wairaka Nazarene church in Jinja, Uganda, is taking care of 12 orphans. Roberta and Betty are the two caregivers. "They are our mothers," one child told me.

These orphans sang three songs for me.

Haunting, mournful, tragic. "We have lost our parents, they are not sitting on the porch or working in the garden . . ."

Hopeful, determined, resilient. "We can do anything if we try, just try, yes we can; stay away from weakness, we can do it . . ."

Timeless, solid truth. "Jesus loves me . . ."

The church's involvement in the lives of these 12 children is giving them hope for a future, something they would not have otherwise. The church has identified 88 other orphans in the immediate community but does not have the resources to assist them materially.

The pastor of nearby Grace Nazarene church has taken in three orphans. "My church also helps orphans in the community with food and clothing," he told me, "but the needs are overwhelming. Please pray for us."

Most churches desperately need seeds and farming

tools for caregivers and school supplies for orphans, like Ngenda Nazarene in Rwanda. They are helping 70 caregivers care for 250 orphans and 5 widows with AIDS by growing peanuts and cassava and raising goats and ducks. But they could use help with seeds and tools. They also provide Christian education in two "classrooms" under trees but struggle to supply needed school materials. Two children have HIV, but they lack funds to test all the children.

Benhilda is a caregiver in Zimbabwe. She had six children who moved to the city; they all died from AIDS. Benhilda's grandchildren, ages 1 to 12, were sent back to her to raise. Benhilda is one of 3,600 beneficiaries that received a food distribution from NCM and Canadian Foodgrains Bank. Elaine Bumstead shares her encounter with Benhilda:

Benhilda looked at me with eyes full of desperation and determination. "I'm teaching my grandchildren to plant vegetables," she said, "but the drought has withered the crops. Thank you for bringing food. We thank God for you." I looked at her frail frame and her legs crippled with arthritis and asked her if she got tired. "I do get tired and lay down," she said, "but the children wake me up. They anxiously ask me if I will die too." She took my hands in hers and said, "I pray to God every morning that He will give me enough days to raise my grandchildren."

Caregivers are the heroes of the African continent. Benhilda is just one of hundreds of thousands of grandmothers across Africa who are struggling to cope with raising their grandchildren on limited or nonexistent incomes. Over and over as I asked what their greatest needs are—food and school fees for the children topped the list.

The Church of the Nazarene is going into the forgotten places "for such a time as this." Sharing their own meager resources, local churches are giving practical help including gardening, babysitting, animal care, carrying firewood and water, community clothing drives, and trying to connect people with health programs as needed. We are the hands of Jesus extended to the suffering.

"The goal of compassionate ministries in Africa," says Trino Jara, "is to move from sponsorship to partnership. By that we mean empowering the needy of Africa to become self-sustaining through help and hope. That's what the AIDS caregivers program does."

An example is Ethiopia where work skills, such as mechanics, agriculture, bee farming, barbering, woodworking, and driver's training, have been offered to 360 caregivers. In countries across Africa, Nazarene churches are coming alongside caregivers with training, support, and love.

"A friend is like a water source for a long journey," says an African proverb. Let us be that friend for caregivers as they pour their lives into the soul care of these precious children.

eight
SOUL
CONTROL

"Wisdom is to the soul what health is to the body" (De Saint-Real).

Population under age 25 in Africa: 71 percent.[18]

* * *

People are lying to our children. And it is killing them.

Never was this more evident than at the 2004 Global AIDS Conference in Thailand. In spite of several major studies done to the contrary, many still insist that the answer to the AIDS crisis is condoms. One session was advertised as a CNN (*C*ondoms, *N*eedles, *N*egotiating skills) vs. ABC (*A*bstinence, *B*e faithful in marriage, *C*ondoms as a last resort) debate. Whenever statements were made that teens cannot be expected to control themselves, or that condoms are proven intervention, there was applause. However, when a woman highlighted the sobering fact that Botswana promoted more condom usage than any other African nation, yet had the second-highest HIV infection rate in the world, she was greeted with booing and catcalls.

"It was incredible to observe the heavy publicity of the condom-producing companies," commented Trino Jara. "Most of the free samples were specially designed for teenagers! Tragically, in the African context condoms are an invitation to young people to practice sex, packaged in the lie that it will be 'safe sex' if they use condoms. Condom promoters refuse to acknowledge their failure rate. They completely ignore the spiritual, emotional, physical, and societal ramifications that are creating tragic results across our continent. The real solution for the millions of teenagers and young adults who are not yet infected is for them to commit to the moral standard of abstinence before marriage and faithfulness in marriage. Only Christ can help them do that, and the Church must lead the way."

> More than half of the estimated 14,000 people newly infected with HIV every day are under 25 years of age.

AIDS is the greatest moral challenge of our time, particularly when it comes to our young people. According to United Nations figures in 2004, more than half of the estimated 14,000 people newly infected with HIV every day are under 25 years of age.

Teenagers face additional behavioral and sociocultural factors that make them more vulnerable to HIV infection. Adolescence is a time when young people typically engage in risk-taking behavior and adventure. Because of emotional immaturity, they are less likely to have lasting relationships and more likely to have multiple partners. For young women, changes in the reproductive tract during puberty make it less resistant to infections. Teens typically struggle with self-esteem; a sexual relationship makes them feel temporarily wanted and loved. For children who have lost parents, selling their bodies may seem their only means of survival.

Many teens in Africa live in areas where there are high rates of crime, violence, poverty, or war. They have no money for fun or entertainment. They feel hopeless and lost about the future. Sex is something they do for a brief respite from the poverty, hunger, and violence that surrounds them every day.

The president of Botswana admitted that the way to turn around the epidemic in his country is for churches to teach abstinence until marriage and faithfulness in marriage.[19] (This is known locally as "zero grazing.")

"The problem is that many of our youth are not hearing this message," said Monte Cyr. "While the Bible often mentions sex, the Church frequently views sex as a personal, forbidden subject. Society blasts our young people with sexual messages from all sides, and very few of these messages agree with God's standards. The Church's silence on such a critical subject can give our youth the mistaken idea that the Church is outdated and irrelevant to their lives.

"As difficult as it might be, the Church must become vocal concerning God's standard: our sexuality is a valuable gift from God to be treasured and given untarnished to our lifelong marriage partner on our wedding day. As we help our young people discover and embrace true holiness, they will come to understand it is a life characterized by honoring God with our choices. Once they truly grasp this, they will understand that sexual behavior must fit into the holiness lifestyle as well."

AIDS training has become a component of camps and youth events across Africa, such as the Festival of Life events held at ANU, attended by hundreds of youth from five countries. Monte also presents specialized workshops on HIV/AIDS. The workshops cover a large amount of information including:

- What AIDS is and how it is transmitted
- What the Bible says about the value of people, our relationships, marriage, and sex
- Sexual peer pressure and how to deal with it
- Cultural practices versus Christian beliefs
- How AIDS impacts our families, our communities, and our churches
- Nutrition and general health
- Discussion of condoms and so-called "safe sex"
- Ten reasons to say no to sex before marriage and a sexual purity pledge

The workshops include small group discussions, movies (*All Affected* and *Choose Freedom*), planning sessions for local church youth groups, drama, question and answer sessions, and stories. It is emphasized that AIDS

Ethiopian poster promoting abstinence

is not always procured through sinful behavior, but if it is, there is forgiveness in Christ.

World Relief has given the Church of the Nazarene permission to reprint its excellent Bible study series called *Choose Life*. The content covers abstinence, morality, purity, and AIDS. Currently it is published in English and Portuguese and is being translated into French, Swahili, and Kinyarwanda.

To illustrate the dangers of reckless sexual behavior, Monte tells the following story about three automobile drivers: The first one breaks the road rules and crashes, killing 7 out of 10 passengers. The second one also crashes, however, since passengers were wearing seat belts, only 4 out of 10 die. The third one obeys the road rules and zero people die. Which automobile would you want to ride in? He tells teens they must choose A, B, C, or D (*A*bstain, *B*e faithful, *C*ommit to Christ, or face *D*eath), and holds up a poster of a body bag with the caption: "Think before you jump in the sack." Ultimately, it is their decision to practice "soul control."

The youth of Africa are responding:

- On the North Kivu District in DRC, a Nazarene high school has an HIV/AIDS club that performs dramas for churches and community groups. The DRC Western District coordinated an HIV/AIDS prevention campaign at the University of Kinshasa.

- A youth ministry team from Namibia has developed a unique repertoire of songs that address the AIDS issue. They perform in local schools, touching the lives of thousands.

- In Rwanda, a Nazarene secondary school of 246 students has an HIV/AIDS club. Through drama, quizzes, and games they help young people become aware of the consequences of choices.

- Zambia South District NYI held a walkathon that raised food donations for an AIDS hospice and an AIDS orphanage.

- "A man propositioned me," shared a teen in the DRC. "He offered to pay my school fees and buy me clothes. Then I remembered the NYI AIDS Conference and my decision to say no to sex before marriage. Even though my father was unemployed, I said no. A month later, God provided my dad with a job, and I was able to return to school."

It's encouraging to know that at the end of 2003, over 90 percent of Africans did *not* have HIV. Young people must be a priority in our efforts. A Swahili proverb says, "A son will be what he is taught." There is much teaching to be done.

Please pray that God would raise up more quality young leaders and provide the needed AIDS ministry resources for them. "Even though AIDS continues to inflict devastation upon Africa," Monte shared, "we are seeing progress. Our training is pointing youth to the only answer for soul control, Jesus Christ!"

nine
SOUL
PROVISION

"Man is so made that when anything fires his soul, impossibilities vanish"
(Jean De La Fontaine).

She was an adorable little African girl walking through a cornfield singing, "This is the day the Lord has made" on an NCM video years ago. Her school principal called her "gifted." Her beautiful voice led a 15-voice youth choir that ministered in churches and local schools. Her mom, Rose, sang in the Wairaka Nazarene church choir until the 2002 Christmas program when she collapsed and died.

Janet got her lovely voice from her mom; sadly, she also got AIDS.

I made arrangements to interview Janet in Uganda. This sweet girl agreed to share with the world God's sustaining grace in the midst of her pain. Then an E-mail informed me that Janet had a stroke and died on Valentine's Day, 2005, at age 16. As I sat weeping at the computer, within moments another E-mail arrived. It was from the NMI book committee, unanimously approving the proposal to tell the story of AIDS in Africa.

O God, please use this story to keep another child's voice from being prematurely stilled.

✳   ✳   ✳

In the time it takes to read this book, more than 300 people will die from AIDS. As you read this single chapter, 120 children will lose a parent to AIDS. Millions more AIDS patients still lie on earthen floors, on mats, on blankets in mud huts or shantytowns or bleak hospital wards all across sub-Saharan Africa. For many of us in the western world, their agony is like a submarine at the bottom of the ocean. We acknowledge the blip on the radar screen, but it is motionless, causing no waves to disturb the comfort of our own journey.

> **In the time it takes to read this book, more than 300 people will die from AIDS.**

The Nazarene church in Africa is doing a great job as it courageously ministers to the overwhelming needs. Yet the Joint United Nations Programme on AIDS (UNAIDS) reports that per capita income for the poorest 25 percent of households in Africa is expected to drop by 13 percent, while at the same time each household can expect to take on four-plus dependents as a result of AIDS. As the Body of Christ, we cannot ignore these distress signals! John Wesley's well-known saying, "the world is my parish," easily translates into global compassionate AIDS ministry outreach. An African proverb says, "The river swells with the contribution of the small streams." Together we can make provision for these precious souls.

Medical personnel can give soul provision.

Nazarene Medical Organization leads medical teams to help with the AIDS crisis. One to Mozambique provided AIDS training for 400 pastors, treated 1,000 patients, and donated $50,000 in medical supplies. Another one to South Africa conducted AIDS workshops in high schools and community centers to 1,500 students. The team also treated 1,600 patients and showed the *JESUS* film.

Dr. Susan Elliott from California volunteered to conduct HIV/AIDS medical training in Zambia. She also spoke at hospitals and clinics on the importance of nutrition for patients and caregivers.

Dr. Mark Redwine from Montana founded SEED (Survival, Education, and Economic Development). SEED is working with 40 churches in Tanzania on a five-year plan of sustainability for AIDS orphans and widows. A unique aspect of their program is that it pairs orphans with widows to form new family units in a cottage setting. SEED has also taken medicines to children in Rwanda and the DRC and given HIV/AIDS training in Burundi.

Universities and churches can give soul provision.

Students at ANU have formulated a list of 23 practical measures to help youth avoid HIV/AIDS and another list of guidelines for compassionately working with people who are HIV positive. Special chapels focus on AIDS. Students from ANU's Religion Student Organization are visiting orphans and collecting food and clothing.

For five years, Trail Church of the Nazarene in New Freedom, Pennsylvania, provided a Christmas newsletter for their congregation of about 100. Members submitted greetings for $3 to $10 with all donations going to AIDS orphans. The average of $150 they raised each year provided enough for two acres of vegetables for a caregiver and her orphans.

Individuals can give soul provision.

God led Pastor Pat Thomas of the Rochester, Minnesota, Nazarene church to create an endowment called Starfish Ministries that would provide care for 1,100 orphans. At $3,000 per child to provide perpetual schooling and basic care, the endowment needs to raise $3.3 million. Starfish Ministries is well on its way with $135,000 already raised.

Rev. Ramby and Karen Campbell were Nazarene missionaries to Malawi and South Africa for eight years until they moved to Kenya. Ramby is project manager for Feed the Children, which partners with Nazarene schools in four of the largest slums in Nairobi. The program feeds 70,000 children every day, many affected by AIDS. Karen volunteers at their Abandoned Baby Center, holding and loving AIDS babies and handicapped children.

After our family traveled to Africa in 2005, our 15-

year-old son, Kevin, sensed God asking him to give up one of his favorite things: our Christmas tree. Instead, our family donated the money to AIDS orphans.

Brian Becker participated in three Point Loma Nazarene University (PLNU) summer teams to Rwanda, Malawi, and Kenya/Uganda. He held an HIV/AIDS awareness workshop at the Nazarene Technical School in Rwanda. Brian worked with the Nazarene pastor who was the citywide leader for HIV/AIDS awareness in Gisenyi. PLNU Malawi team leader Kelly Tirrill shared, "We wanted to be more consistent with the gospel by being a part of the worldwide work of the Church with the AIDS pandemic."

✳ ✳ ✳

The Nazarene infrastructure and volunteers allow AIDS ministries to be very cost effective when carried out by local churches. We have systems of feedback and accountability in place. Outcomes are concrete and measurable: children fed and clothed, schools built and children educated, crops improved, microfinance and vocational jobs started, people led to the Lord. There is a popular billboard in Africa that reads, "Anyone can catch AIDS but everyone can prevent it." We can *all* do something!

What Will I Do?

Dr. Samuel Hynd served for over 55 years in a variety of medical ministries in Swaziland. He was awarded

Dr. Samuel Hynd

the Royal Order of Sobhuza II in 1989 and the Comman-
der of the British Empire by Queen Elizabeth in London
in 1999. At 80, Dr. Hynd was still working 10- to 12-hour
days in a clinic where almost half his patients have
HIV/AIDS. As Dr. Hynd was helping a nurse take down
an IV drip from a man with AIDS, the needle, with the

patient's blood still on it, swung around and lodged in his finger. He immediately cleaned out the needle prick and began a course of antiretroviral drugs. Fortunately he has tested negative for HIV.

In August 2004 he was robbed and stabbed multiple times. After receiving stitches and filing a report with the police, Dr. Hynd returned to care for his patients until 9:30 that night. His motivating scripture is, "Heal the sick, raise the dead, cleanse those who have leprosy, drive out demons. Freely you have received, freely give" (Matt. 10:8).

Dr. Hynd tells a story about a woman with AIDS who said, "I've taken all the treatments, the pills, the injections, but I know I'm dying. Can someone just hold me as I die?"

While Dr. Hynd shares that he's working harder than he ever has, he indicates that he can't get away from her looking-for-hope words.

He asks himself: *What will I do to help hold each person with AIDS? To give soul provision so they can say, "Someone loved me as I died?"* And the answer comes back: *Whatever I can do, with whatever means I have.*

We can ask, "What would Jesus do?" or "What would John Wesley do?" or even "What is the Church of the Nazarene doing?" But the ultimate spiritual question is, "What will I do?"

ten
SOUL
MATES

"I sought my soul, but my soul I could not see.
I sought my God, but my God eluded me. I
sought my brother and I found all three"
(source unknown).

That old Nazarene Bible College used to have a power coming from it!" exclaimed the young Zulu man. "There was a power we could feel there."

"That power is the Holy Spirit," Derek Liebenberg told him. "Last Sunday we prayed and invited the Holy Spirit to once again take control. Tell your friends the power is back!"

❊   ❊   ❊

In July 2003 a young Nazarene couple named Derek and Heather Liebenberg answered the question, "What will I do?" They raised their own support and moved from Canada to South Africa to help with the AIDS crisis. A study of the greater Durban area showed that the most needy area was Bhekulwandle, which in Zulu means "ocean view." The Liebenbergs also heard that a former Nazarene Bible College was in Bhekulwandle. They accompanied retired farmer Rob Gill in delivering emergency food rations to those in the last stages of AIDS, the orphans, and widows. "Every home we went to was within sight of that former Nazarene college," shared Derek. "And every home we visited had at least one fresh grave. Some had three. Heather and I knew this was where God wanted us."

The Bible college had been abandoned in the early 1990s because of heavy fighting during apartheid. Over the years the sewage had backed up, rooms were used as "barns" for goats, every window was broken out, the yard was vastly overgrown, and squatters had moved in. Undaunted, Derek sought permission to use the building as an AIDS Center. He registered the ministry under the name Mercy Economic Development of South Africa (MEDSA) and called it "Center of Hope."

Youth from the Bhekulwandle and Calvary Nazarene churches and many other volunteers helped clean, paint, and install burglar bars and steel doors. In August 2003 a dedication service was held at the Bhekulwandle Nazarene church. The "power" was back.

It was not long before Derek and Heather discovered that, for those devastated by AIDS, hope emerges as the primary need. "On our second visitation with Rob," said Derek, "all of the chronically ill we visited the previous month were dead except one, a young man lying outside his hut. He was a human skeleton barely able to lift his hand. It was very moving to be with someone so close to a potentially Christless eternity. As Rob Gill explained the gospel to him and prayed with the family, I thought that this was one of the most unselfish forms of evangelism I had ever encountered. There are no new names for membership rolls, no increase in tithes as a result, not even a very long window for discipleship. It is quite literally 'snatching souls from hell.'"

They also soon discovered what an amazing difference some rice, corn meal, beans, and salt can make. People listless one month are up and walking the next. Clearly nutrition is important. "People who are dying from AIDS, malnourished and hungry, are within sight of the resort beaches and restaurants in Durban," commented Derek. "It is a microcosm of the global situation and makes us realize the consumer culture we have become accustomed to. The people in Bhekulwandle are teaching us to never forget how others live."

Soon they organized a Bhekulwandle community task force. Volunteers began with a structured children's program on Tuesdays and Thursdays. The program, called Simunye Time (We Are One), has Bible stories, drama, singing, and soccer. Donated basketball hoops inspired an all-star team. A local businessman donates a hot meal for 200 children every week, delivered by a dedicated man from Chatsworth Nazarene. Friday's activities are just for fun. Their favorite is the slip and slide. With a simple piece of plastic, water, and lathered soap, the kids have a laughing, bubbly, exuberant time of getting clean.

Seven-year-old Thabiso came regularly to Simunye Time, but he never smiled. He often rested every few steps, breathing heavily and with difficulty. Concerned, Simunye children's workers went to visit his family, only to discover the entire family had died from AIDS. They took Thabiso to the hospital where he was diagnosed with advanced tuberculosis. When filling out the paperwork, volunteer Karen Pretorius was asked to pick a birth date for Thabiso since his was unknown. When he got well, Karen gave Thabiso the first birthday celebration he'd ever had. He got a balloon, milkshake, and birthday cake. "When I took Thabiso's picture that day," reflected Derek, "it was the first time I ever saw him smile."

Center of Hope has been blessed with volunteers. Kelly-Ann Snyders led Simunye Time for a year and mentored a local resident. Twice a month Collette Snyders teaches art. Calvary Nazarene volunteers Lorraine and Keith teach AIDS patients how to manufacture products, such as trays and candles. Professional dressmaker Jenny teaches sewing.

An after-school program began in April 2004 to help children with their academics. The fatherless children have a tremendous need for role models in their lives; male Bible teachers disciple boys who receive Christ.

Pat Magula, a pastor's wife, leads the AIDS counseling ministries. One day two young women came to Center of Hope, one of them with infant twins. They were exhausted, disheveled, and desperate. When their family had heard they were HIV positive, they denied them food, saying, "You are dying anyway, why should we waste our food on you?"

"We read Scripture and prayed, fed them, and let them pick out some clothes," shared Derek. "The next day they returned, not to ask for anything, but to thank us. They said we were the first people who touched them since they had told people their HIV status. They asked us how they could love like us, and Pat led them to Christ that very day."

Children's Aid International Relief and Development partnered with MEDSA in 2004. They provided security gates and bars, window glass, administrative support, a small truck, a salary for a full-time Zulu teacher, and financial support for the children's program. The South Africa Booksmart Foundation donated hundreds of children's books. Two local doctors volunteer for two hours a week. Children are tested for scabies, ringworm, intestinal difficulties, poor nutrition, and other minor ailments. They hope soon to have the capability to test for AIDS.

One elderly grandmother is caring for 15 grandchildren, one of them severely handicapped, on her pension of just R742 (U.S. $120) per month. Situations like this prompted the decision to begin "door gardens." These plots are literally the size of a household door, easily manageable for elderly folks or children. Heather teaches how to dig holes, compost, and plant.

The Zulu king, Goodwill Zwelithini, met with Derek

King Zwelithini cutting the ribbon at Center of Hope. Derek is standing to the right, in the center.

and Heather to express appreciation for their ministry and in January 2005 formally opened Center of Hope. They also met former South African president Nelson Mandela. Yet the work has not been without its challenges: robbed repeatedly, windows smashed over 20 times, and the center set on fire twice. (Fortunately local Nazarenes put out the fires before serious damage was done.)

The day of the first fire, Center of Hope was ministering in the local school. Volunteer John Forbes gave his testimony of living with AIDS and Christ's transforming power. Praise Nkosi preached, and almost 200 prayed to receive Christ.

"The fire was set deliberately, but we are not discouraged," Derek shared. "God used a fire to call Moses to rescue his people from bondage in Egypt. Today He is still calling His people to enter enemy territory and lead the people out of the bondage of poverty, disease, ignorance, crime, hatred, and sin. God told Moses, 'I have indeed seen the misery of my people . . . I have heard them crying . . . and I am concerned about their suffering' (Exod. 3:7). We believe He is saying the same today about people suffering from AIDS."

Death is all around us. It has a look, a feel, a smell.

Some days that suffering is very real. "Death is all around us," Derek wrote in 2004. "It has a look, a feel, a smell. I am sitting in the casualty ward of the local hospital. The emaciated body of two-year-old Zandile is breaking my heart. She can barely open her sunken eyes. Next to me sits her *gogo* (grandmother). Robbed of her children by this killer disease, all she has left is Zandile and her older sister who is in our Simunye Time program. Gogo is normally a cheerful, consistent soul who has borne up under a lifetime of suffering. But tonight she is old, gray, tired. Her shoulders hunched, face to the floor, she is well acquainted with the sorrow and grief that lies before her like a dark tunnel through which she must pass again. I am a grim witness to this catastrophic and devastating disease. When will the Church rise up and respond to this tragedy?"

Zandile died the next day.

That Sunday Derek and Paul and Pat Magula went up the rutted dirt track to the grandmother's simple mud house. They paid their respects and began to sing in Zulu. Derek, discouraged, gazed wearily out the doorway to the hill in the distance. "Suddenly I realized that I was looking at the Center of Hope building from the broken plastic chair on which I sat. What an awesome responsibility God has given us to have a ministry within sight of people dying, grieving, and starving. If there is anything needed in the face of human misery, it is hope."

The Tswana of South Africa have a proverb, "To give away is to make provision for the future." Volunteers and living month to month by faith, this young couple has chosen to give away their lives to be soul mates to those suffering from AIDS in Africa. Some have told them that they are wasting their time trying to stem the tide. Yet darkness only causes a light to be more visible, more effective, and more intense. Because of Christ, Derek and Heather hold their flickering candles in the darkness of Bhekulwandle, and believe: "The people walking in darkness have seen a great light; on those living in the land of the shadow of death, a light has dawned" (Isa. 9:2).

* * *

It was with great shock and sadness to hear that on December 28, 2005, Derek suffered a sudden heart attack and went to be with our Lord. Just 40, Derek was anticipating the long-awaited birth of his first child in April 2006.

As we worked on this story earlier in 2005, Derek wrote: "I believe that we must present Jesus personally to this generation, to mobilize as many as possible to help in this task, and to train and equip believers for their part in fulfilling both the Great Commission and the Great Commandment. Imagine a billion candles blazing out, defying the deathly darkness. May the Lord make us truly the light of the world!"

Heather and her son are valiantly continuing the inspiring work at Center of Hope.

EPILOGUE
bless the lord, o my soul

"The windows of my soul
I throw wide open to the sun"
(John Greenleaf Whittier, "My Psalm").

The door was just a torn piece of cloth. Inside the tiny, dark room was a lean world reduced to simple objects: newspapers plastered on mud walls, a thin slice of foam on the dirt floor, a single bowl, a handful of food. Esther's home, the place she will die. Bedridden with AIDS, Esther has nothing of this world except friends from Wairaka Church of the Nazarene who have been visiting her. Today as we pray with her, Esther chooses to accept a gift: Jesus.

Her radiance lightens the room, welcomes grace to the reality.

❋   ❋   ❋

I am sitting on the white sands of Zanzibar, an island off the east coast of Africa. My view is a dazzling vista of palm trees burnished by golden sun and the endless sapphire ocean. It is a tropical palette of paradise.

I have written: "I believe it is the soul that makes a person beautiful." I think of my Christian African friends

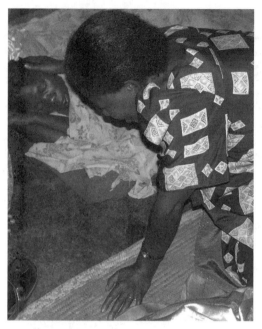

Pastor Irene praying for Esther

dying with AIDS. Wispy hair. Thin bones. Hardly skin or flesh left. They are so beautiful.

I smile when I think of their Paradise to come.

Grains of soft white sand sift through my fingers. Job's misery outweighed the sand of the seas (Job 6:3). Africa's misery, AIDS, crushes and suffocates. Yet God gave Solomon wisdom as measureless as the sand on the seashore (1 Kings 4:29). God help us, we beg.

I study the vast turquoise horizon. Thinking. In the Good Samaritan story, Jesus asked the expert of the Law which of the three men was a neighbor to the beaten man. I imagine understanding dawning as he breathed, "The one who had mercy on him."

Someone once said, "Love looks not with the eyes but with the soul." I like to think the Good Samaritan saw with his soul, that place in each of us where compassion is birthed and gives life to acts of mercy.

The Good Samaritan is like the Zulu proverb, "The one who walks me through the night is the one I remember in the morning." When Jesus said, "Go and do likewise," He was instructing us to walk through this darkness called AIDS with our global neighbors, the widows and orphans of Africa.

We are the Church of the Nazarene. We stand at the threshold of an astonishing opportunity to minister to millions of people. They are living with AIDS in the very communities where our churches already are.

Africa's soul hope lies in our hands, in our influences, in our prayers, in our resources.

Have mercy.

CALL TO ACTION
soul engagement

"We are here for the sake of others, for the countless unknown souls with whose future we are connected by a bond of compassion" (Albert Einstein).

For more information on AIDS, check the following Internet sites:

< www.praytoendaids.com >

< www.unaids.org >

< www.aegis.com >

< www.aids.org >

< www.knowhivaids.org >

< http://pandemicfacingaids.org >

< www.ccih.org >

- Contact NCM for AIDS resources: < www.ncm .org > .
- For information about a documentary film about AIDS in Swaziland called *Dear Francis,* go to < www.dearfrancis.org > .
- Invite speakers, particularly people living with AIDS, to address your group or at a churchwide fellowship meal.
- Urge your pastor to preach on the AIDS pandemic and compassionate outreach.

- Participate in Global AIDS Day each year (December 1), perhaps even joining with other local congregations in your community.
- The third Sunday in May is the International AIDS Candlelight Memorial. Plan a worship service that focuses on a compassionate response to those with AIDS.
- Contact your local media and encourage them to have greater coverage of HIV/AIDS. Use AIDS Action Alert, which makes it easy to contact local newspapers: < www.aidsaction.org >.
- Fast a meal to pray for those who are suffering, and/or fast from a recreational activity and donate the saved funds to NCM for AIDS ministries.
- Write letters to encourage people living with HIV/AIDS. Establish a care team to visit those with AIDS.
- World Relief has an excellent three-part Sunday School series on AIDS in Africa. Use this free resource to encourage involvement.
- Publish a list of legislators who make policy and budget decisions about AIDS research and assistance funding. Encourage your congregation to contact them.
- Provide School Pal-Paks, used clothing, and Crisis Care Kits (see NCM web site for instructions).

Pray for:

- The Africa Region and the many challenges it faces
- Those dying from AIDS, that they may find Christ
- Nazarene Compassionate Ministries
- Training for pastors and leaders
- Abstinence workshops and training for youth
- Wisdom for materials to train local congregations in the care of people infected with and affected by AIDS
- Caregivers and their needs, such as seeds, tools, and animals, to start small gardens for orphans
- The physical and educational needs of AIDS orphans
- Those who minister and provide vocational training for AIDS orphans

"Don't let what you cannot do tear you from what you can do" (Ghana proverb).

PRONUNCIATION GUIDE

The following information will assist in pronouncing some unfamiliar words in this book. The suggested pronunciations, though not always precise, are close approximations of the way the terms are pronounced.

Acknowledgments and Prologue

Kruger	KROO-ger
Marungu	mah-ROON-goo
Musimbi	moo-SEEM-bee
Schmelzenbach	SHMEHL-zhuhn-bah
silumu	see-LOO-moo
Siyabonga kakhulu	see-yah-BOHN-gah kah-KOO-loo
Wairaka	yie-RAHK-uh

Chapter 1

Hynd	HIND
Katindo	kah-TEEN-doh
Lesotho	luh-SOO-too
Magagula	mah-gah-GOO-lah
Manzini	mahn-ZEE-nee
Menya	MAYN-yah
Ushindi	oo-SHEEN-dee

Chapter 2

Aliba, Petua	ah-LEE-bah peh-TOO-ah
Chewa	CHAY-wah
kulowa kufa	koo-LOH-wah KOO-fah
Mwanza, Mwabi	mm-WAHN-zah mm-WAH-bee
Yao	Yahoh

Chapter 3

Bakasa   bah-KAH-sah
Kaunda   kah-OON-dah
Malinzi   mah-LEEN-zee
Maputo   mah-POO-toh
Mokebe   moh-KAY-bee
Pato   PAH-toh
Obotte   oh-BOH-tay
Togolese   TOH-goh-leez
Tsambe   TSAHM-bay
Tshembeka   tsehm-BEH-kah

Chapter 4

Mavuso   mah-VOO-soh
Mswati   mm-SWAH-tee
Tinkundla   teen-KOON-dlah
Shongwe, Cariot   SHOHNG-way KEH-ree-uht

Chapter 5

Anastasis   an-uh-STAY-sis
Côte d'Ivoire   KOHT Dee-VWAHR
Cyr   SEER
Goma   GOH-mah
Mzuzu   mm-ZOO-Zoo
Jara, Trino   HAH-rah TREE-noh
Salamba   sah-LAHM-bah

Chapter 6

Désiré, Bugeshi   deh-zih-RAY boo-GAY-shee
Fanual   FAN-yoo-ehl
Kagarama   kah-gah-RAH-mah
Kisumu   kee-SOO-moo
Netsai   NEHT-sie
Ngoma   nn-GOH-mah
Oketch   oh-KEHTCH
Pindile   pihn-DEE-leh

Chapter 7

Jinja	JIHN-juh
Kibadawa	kee-bah-DAH-wah
Ngenda	nn-GEHN-dah
ugali	oo-GAH-lee

Chapter 8

Kinyarwanda	keen-yahr-WAHN-dah
Kivu	KEE-voo
Swahili	swah-HEE-lee

Chapter 9

Ginsenyi	geh-SEHN-yeh

Chapter 10

Bhekulwandle	beh-kool-WAHN-dleh
gogo	GOH-goh
Liebenberg	LEE-behn-berg
Mandela	mahn-DEH-lah
Magula	mah-GOO-lah
Nkosi	nn-KOH-see
Pretorius	pree-TOH-ree-us
Simunye	sih-MOON-yuh
Thabiso	tah-BEE-soh
Tswana	TSWAH-nah
Zadile	zah-DEE-leh
Zwelithini	zweh-lee-TEE-nee

NOTES:

1. < www.knowhivaids.org > , 2004

2. Fact sheet 2002: The USG response to Swaziland's HIV and AIDS epidemic Feb. 1, 2002 (US Embassy in the Kingdom of Swaziland) < http://usembassy.state.gov/posts/wz1/wwwh hivfsheet.html > .

3. World Health Organization, UNAIDS, 2001

4. *Christian Science Monitor,* November 4, 2004

5. Reuters, March 4, 2004

6. World Bank Report, December 22, 2004

7. UNAIDS

8. UNICEF, 2003

9. World Bank, September 2004

10. UNICEF: United for Children, October, 2005

11. Basildon Peta, *London Independent,* November 26, 2003

12. < http://news.bbc.co.uk/2/hi/africa/4317019.stm >

13. UN Development Program, 2004

14. UNAIDS, 2004

15. UNAIDS and WHO, AIDS Epidemic Update, December, 2004

16. UNICEF: United for Children, October, 2005

17. Ibid.

18. *National Geographic,* September 2005

19. < http://news.bbc.co.uk/1/hi/talking_point /3223194.stm >